LOS ANGELES LAKERS

by Marty Gitlin

Printed in the United States of America,
North Mankato, Minnesota
062011
092011

 THIS BOOK CONTAINS AT LEAST 10% RECYCLED MATERIALS.

Editor: J Chris Roselius
Copy Editor: Anna Comstock
Series design and cover production: Christa Schneider
Interior production: Carol Castro

Photo Credits: Rich Schultz/AP Images, cover; Kevork Djansezian/AP Images, 1; AP Images, 4, 11, 12, 21, 25, 29, 42 (top, middle, bottom), 43 (top); Wen Roberts/NBAE/Getty Images, 7; RBK/AP Images, 8; Matty Zimmerman/AP Images, 15; Harry Harris/AP Images, 17; HPM/AP Images, 18; Wen Roberts/ NBAE/Getty Images, 22; Jim Cummins/NBAE/Getty Images, 26; Focus on Sports/Getty Images, 30; Bob Galbraith/AP Images, 33, 43 (middle); Jim Mone/ AP Images, 34; Jim Rogash/AP Images, 36; Mark J. Terrill/AP Images, 39, 43 (bottom); Michael Dwyer/AP Images, 41; Kim Johnson Flodin/AP Images, 44; Danny Moloshok/AP Images, 47

Library of Congress Cataloging-in-Publication Data
Gitlin, Marty.
  Los Angeles Lakers / by Marty Gitlin.
    p. cm. -- (Inside the NBA)
  Includes index.
  ISBN 978-1-61783-161-4
  1. Los Angeles Lakers (Basketball team)--History--Juvenile literature. I. Title.
  GV885.52.L67G57 2012
  796.323'640979494--dc23
                              2011021808

TABLE OF CONTENTS

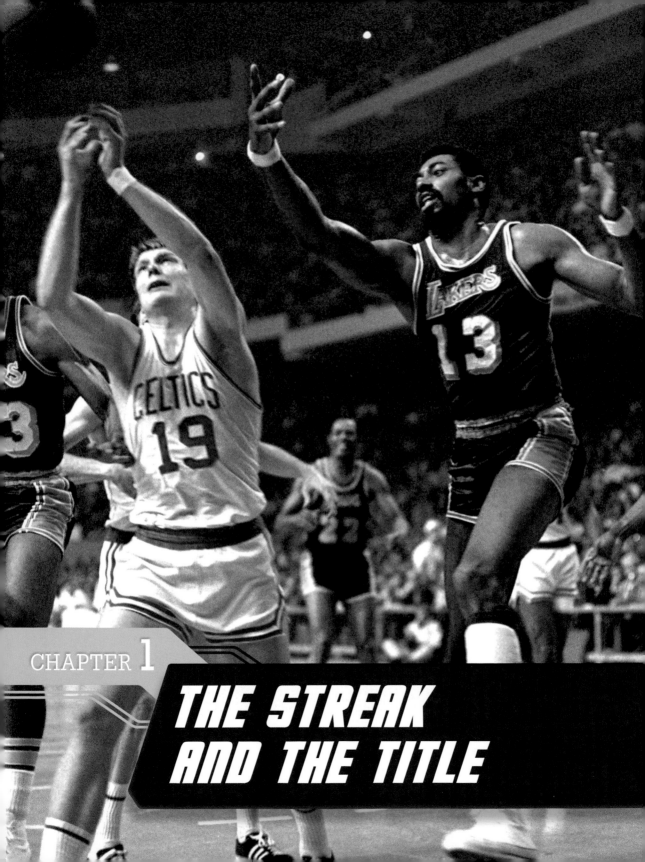

CHAPTER 1

THE STREAK AND THE TITLE

On October 31, 1971, the Los Angeles Lakers of the National Basketball Association (NBA) lost an early regular-season game to the Golden State Warriors 109–105. The Lakers fell to 6–3 with the loss. That defeat would be the last one Los Angeles would suffer for more than two months.

Los Angeles played 33 games between November 5 and January 7, and won all of them.

Glancing at the Lakers' 1971–72 roster, it is easy to guess why such a winning streak was possible. The team started the year with three of the greatest players in NBA history in center Wilt Chamberlain, guard Jerry West, and forward Elgin Baylor. Even more remarkable, all three players were at least 33 years old and well past their primes.

Los Angeles center Wilt Chamberlain (13) fights Don Nelson (19) of Boston for a rebound.

MR. CLUTCH

The Lakers have arguably featured more star players in their history than any other franchise. The best Lakers player ever could very well have been guard Jerry West. The 14-time All-Star finished his career averaging 27 points per game and was among the finest defensive guards in NBA history. He was also known for rising to the occasion. That earned him the nickname "Mr. Clutch."

"He is the master," praised Celtics guard Larry Siegfried after West was named 1969 NBA Finals Most Valuable Player (MVP). "He is the only guard."

After retiring as a player, West served as the Lakers' coach in the late 1970s and later as their general manager. He became President of Basketball Operations for the Memphis Grizzlies in 2002.

In fact, Baylor played only the first nine games that season before retiring.

Still, the Lakers appeared unstoppable. They not only featured Chamberlain and West, but they also had floppy-haired guard Gail Goodrich. He was one of the finest shooters in the game. As such, he led the Lakers in scoring at 25.9 points per game. Forwards Jim McMillian and Happy Hairston rounded out an almost unstoppable starting lineup.

But then came January 9, 1972. The Lakers were traveling to Wisconsin to play the defending NBA champion Milwaukee Bucks. Chamberlain would be matched up against Kareem Abdul-Jabbar. The young post player had taken Chamberlain's distinction of being the league's premier center. If the Lakers

Jerry West (44) of the Los Angeles Lakers dribbles past Herm Gilliam (9) of the Buffalo Braves during a game in 1971.

were going to lose a game, this could be it.

It was a Sunday afternoon. A national television audience settled in to witness the showdown. And they watched as the Bucks scored 12 straight points in the fourth quarter to cruise to a 120–104 victory. The Lakers' 33-game winning streak had come to an end. But it remained the longest in NBA history through the 2010–11 season.

The Lakers missed three foul shots during Milwaukee's 12–0 fourth-quarter run. They also missed some easy shots from the floor. That led McMillian to say, "I guess we got caught up in all the excitement."

But McMillian and the Lakers realized more excitement would come their way.

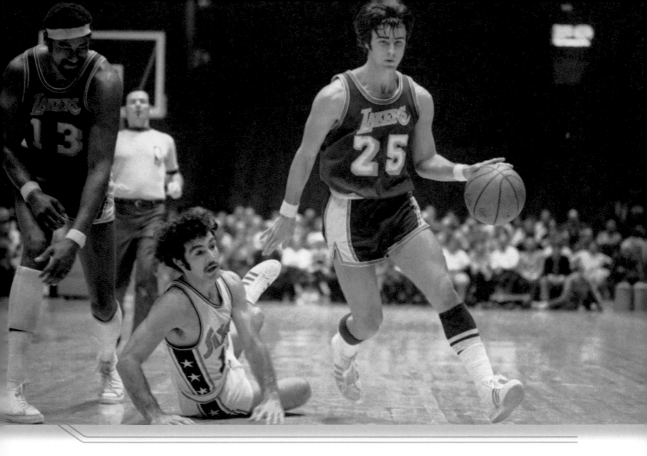

Gail Goodrich (25) of the Lakers dribbles past Dave Wohl (13) of the Philadelphia 76ers in 1971.

Steamroller!

The Lakers did not just beat opponents during their 33-game winning streak in 1971–72. They dominated them. They scored an amazing 123.3 points per game. And their average margin of victory was 16 points per game. Among their victims were the Milwaukee Bucks, who later halted the streak. The Lakers beat the Bucks in Los Angeles, 112–105, to extend it to 11 in a row.

They knew they would have a chance for revenge against Milwaukee in the playoffs. The two teams were clearly the best in the NBA's Western Conference. The Lakers finished the season at 69–13. At the time, that was the finest regular-season record in NBA history. Los Angeles beat the Chicago Bulls easily in the opening round of the playoffs to force a showdown against the Bucks in the conference finals.

The Lakers had scored at least 100 points in every game but one during the regular season. So when they lost Game 1 at home to Milwaukee, 93–72, some believed they were in trouble. But McMillian scored 42 points in a thrilling 135–134 Game 2 victory for Los Angeles. Chamberlain then held Abdul-Jabbar scoreless in the last 10 minutes of Game 3 to secure the Lakers' second win. Los Angeles went on to win the series in six games to set up a clash for the NBA title against the New York Knicks.

Los Angeles followed a similar path in the Finals. The Lakers played poorly and lost Game 1. But they regrouped and won four straight, clinching the title. They had earned

Rebounding Machine

Toward the end of his career, Wilt Chamberlain was no longer the high scorer he had once been. But Chamberlain could still rebound. He averaged 18.6 rebounds per game to lead the league in 1972–73, his last season before retiring. During his 14-year career, he led the NBA in rebounding 11 times.

their first NBA championship since 1954, when they still played in Minneapolis. In the title-clinching Game 5, Chamberlain recorded 24 points and 29 rebounds.

During the 17-year period between championships, the Lakers lost in the Finals eight times. West had experienced seven of those defeats, so he was thrilled to have finally won.

"It's an unbelievable feeling, something I've always wanted to experience," he said. "Now I know what it feels like to be a champion."

West believed he would experience the same thrill the following season. The Lakers steamrolled to a 60–22 record in 1972–73, but were not the same offensive power as they had been the previous year. They averaged 10 fewer points per game that season. In a rematch of the 1972 NBA Finals, the Knicks' stifling defense proved too strong for Los Angeles. The Knicks won the last four games of the series.

The 1972 Finals series marked the end of Chamberlain's career. West would retire a year later. Ironically, the Lakers would soon replace Chamberlain with Abdul-Jabbar. But despite those two players' success at center, older basketball fans remembered quite well when the Lakers once boasted the NBA's first superstar center.

That legendary center wore a Lakers uniform when the team played in Minneapolis. His name was George Mikan.

Jim McMillian (5) of Los Angeles chases after Earl Monroe of the New York Knicks after Monroe grabbed a loose ball during a game in 1973.

CHAPTER 2

FIVE FAST TITLES, BY GEORGE!

Building a championship team usually takes time. But the Minneapolis Lakers dominated professional basketball before and after the NBA was born.

They joined the National Basketball League (NBL) for the 1947–48 season. That same year, the Professional Basketball League of America (PBLA) was founded. But the PBLA failed and folded within a month. Its players were distributed around the NBL. And the Lakers landed a center named George Mikan.

Mikan had already led the Chicago American Gears to an NBL championship in 1946–47. He then led the Lakers to the title in their first season, 1947–48. The following season, the Lakers joined the Basketball Association of America (BAA). Mikan again led them to that crown. During the offseason in 1949, the BAA merged into the

Center George Mikan (99) of the Minneapolis Lakers grabs a rebound in front of guard Herman Schaefer (10) against the Washington Capitols in 1949.

THE "MIKAN RULE"

"How can we stop George Mikan?" That was the question many NBA opponents asked in the early 1950s.

At the time, players were allowed in the lane in front of the basket for only three seconds at a time. So in 1951, the NBA Rules Committee widened the lane, a rule many people believe was created to slow down Mikan. The narrow lanes had allowed Mikan to step away, and then quickly return close to the basket.

The Rochester Royals' coach, Les Harrison, loved the rule change.

Author Michael Schumacher wrote, "As far as Harrison was concerned, the Royals' fast-paced . . . style of basketball was wasted on a team like the Minneapolis Lakers. They were slow, plodding and dull, thanks mainly to the big guy who ambled up the court and then proceeded to beat the living daylights out of his competition."

NBA, and Mikan again led the Lakers to the first championship in that league in 1950.

Mikan was an outstanding scorer. In 1949–50, he averaged 27.4 points per game during an NBA season in which only one other player averaged more than 20. He also averaged 31.3 points per game in the playoffs.

Mikan's strong play against the Syracuse Nationals in the first NBA Finals helped lead the Lakers to the title. The Lakers won Game 1 on a 40-foot shot by guard Bob Harrison as the final second ticked off the clock. The Nationals evened the series by winning Game 2. But the Lakers then won three of the next four games to take the title.

The 6-foot-10 Mikan did more than score. He led the NBA in rebounds the next two seasons, helping lead

Forward Vern Mikkelsen (19) of the Minneapolis Lakers shoots during a game against the New York Knicks in 1953.

Minneapolis back to the finals in 1952. There, he and the Lakers were tested by the New York Knicks. But Mikan recorded 22 points and 19 rebounds in the deciding Game 7 to clinch another championship. After the 82–65 victory, the crowd of 8,600 fans at the Minneapolis Auditorium stormed the court in celebration.

They would also celebrate in 1953 and 1954, when their Lakers would again beat the Knicks and then the Nationals to win their sixth title in seven

Marvelous Mikkelsen

It was not easy to emerge from behind the shadow of the great George Mikan. But Lakers forward Vern Mikkelsen did just that. Mikkelsen forged a Hall of Fame career of his own. He averaged 14.4 points and 9.4 rebounds per game during his 10-year career. He also earned six trips to the NBA All-Star Game.

years. And they had Mikan to thank for it.

"He was the greatest impact player of that era," said Boston Celtics Hall of Fame guard Bob Cousy. "He was a big man who could do so many things on the court."

Mikan did not carry the Lakers by himself. Forward Vern Mikkelsen developed into one of the premier scorers and rebounders in the NBA. But when Mikan retired in 1954 to become the team's general manager, the Lakers needed a great player to take his place. And they got one in young center Clyde Lovellette.

Lovellette scored and rebounded well. But he struggled to play good defense. The Lakers continued to win, but not enough to maintain their dynasty. Starting in 1955–56, Minneapolis would suffer six straight losing seasons.

Not a Chip off the Old Block

The son of early Lakers superstar George Mikan also played in the NBA. But he did not play nearly as well as his father. Larry Mikan was a little-used forward for the Cleveland Cavaliers. He played in only one season and averaged just three points per game.

The Lakers tried everything to improve. Mikan even came out of retirement to play for a short time. He also became the head coach at the start of the 1957–58 season. But he resigned when the team's record fell to a shocking 9–30. Minneapolis finished the season in last place.

But that terrible record had a silver lining. It allowed the Lakers to select first overall in the 1958 college draft. The club chose a forward named Elgin Baylor.

Baylor averaged 24.9 points and 15 rebounds per game to

Elgin Baylor of the Minneapolis Lakers jumps up to score against the New York Knicks in 1958.

earn Rookie of the Year honors and lead the Lakers into the playoffs. The league's newest superstar then led his team to a stunning upset of the St. Louis Hawks in the Western Conference finals. But the Lakers soon lost to the Boston Celtics in the NBA Finals.

The next season, 1959–60, did not go as well for Minneapolis. Baylor averaged 29.6 points and 16.4 rebounds per game, but the Lakers finished just 25–50. They also finished their run in Minneapolis. They were about to move to sunny California.

CHAPTER 3

GREATNESS AND FRUSTRATION

I n the late 1950s, attendance at Lakers games in Minneapolis was dwindling. So team owner Bob Short transferred his team to Los Angeles in 1960.

The Lakers had a new home. They also had a new superstar in Jerry West to team up with Elgin Baylor. West would become one of the greatest guards to ever play in the NBA. Together, Baylor and West overwhelmed opponents. They combined to score an incredible 69.1 points per game during the 1961–62 season to

Shortchanged?

Bob Short twice moved a team he owned to a new town. Short took over as the Minneapolis Lakers' owner in 1957. The team was bad and so was attendance. In February 1960, the Lakers played two games in Los Angeles. Short permanently moved the team there the following season. Later, in 1972, Short angered the baseball fans of Washington DC by moving their Senators to Texas.

The Los Angeles Lakers' Jerry West drives around Chicago Bulls players in a 1968 playoff game.

SUPER FOR HIS SIZE

It is ironic that the Lakers' 33-game winning streak during the 1971–72 season began the day Elgin Baylor retired. They probably could not have won without him during his prime.

Baylor was incredibly strong, and he was a great rebounder for a player who was only 6-foot-5. He not only averaged 27.4 points per game during his career, but he had an average of 13.5 rebounds per game, as well. Baylor was at his best from 1960 to 1963, when he averaged an astounding 35 points and 17 rebounds per game.

"He is without a doubt one of the truly great players to play this game," said teammate and fellow Hall of Famer Jerry West. "He had that wonderful, magical instinct for making plays, for doing things that you just had to watch. . . . It was incredible to watch Elgin play."

lead the Lakers into the NBA Finals.

They were up against Boston with a title on the line. A key steal and basket by West gave the Lakers a 117–115 victory in Game 3. Baylor then scored an NBA playoff-record 61 points to secure a win in Game 5. The Lakers lost badly in Game 6 to set up a one-game showdown for the title.

Lakers guard Frank Selvy tried to play the role of hero in Game 7. He made two baskets, tying the score late in the fourth quarter. He then had a chance to win the game in the final seconds. He shot a baseline jumper about eight feet from the basket. It was a shot he had made hundreds of times before, but the ball bounced off the rim as time expired.

Los Angeles then lost in overtime 110–107. The Lakers

Elgin Baylor of the Lakers drives in for a hook shot in the fourth period of a 1962 NBA Finals game against the Boston Celtics.

could not figure out how to slow down Bill Russell. The Celtics' center scored 30 points and grabbed 40 rebounds in that final game. The defeat was devastating.

Jerry West (44) of the Lakers goes up for a layup against the Baltimore Bullets.

"I would trade all my points for that last basket," Selvy said after the game.

But the Lakers were upset about more than the missed shot that would have secured an NBA championship.

"Selvy thought Bob Cousy fouled him," Baylor said. "I thought Cousy fouled him. . . .

I was in a position to get the offensive rebound. But somebody behind me shoved me out of bounds right into the referee. There was no call there either."

The battle between the Celtics and the Lakers in the 1962 Finals was the start of one of the greatest rivalries in the NBA. It was a rivalry the Celtics dominated during the 1960s.

West scored at least 25 points per game in each of the next 10 seasons. Baylor averaged 24 points and 10 rebounds per game in seven of the next eight seasons. But the Lakers were basically a two-man team—they had little depth. The Celtics had Russell, and they were also a deeper squad. Boston and Los Angeles faced each other six times in the NBA Finals in the 1960s. The Celtics won all six of those Finals.

For years, the Lakers could only wonder what could have

Not Funny to Frank

The Los Angeles Times *reported in 2010 that former Lakers teammate "Hot Rod" Hundley had been playing a joke on Frank Selvy for years. Hundley would call Selvy on the phone and say, "Nice shot, Frank," and then hang up. He was referring to Selvy's missed shot that could have won Game 7 of the 1962 Finals.*

been if Selvy's shot in 1962 had dropped through the net. Some believe it would have changed the course of NBA history and paved the way for more Los Angeles titles.

"We were one shot away from changing the entire history of pro basketball," said Lakers forward Tommy Hawkins. "And it didn't happen for us."

Russell was close to retirement by the time Los Angeles obtained a center to counter him. In 1968, the Lakers traded three players and cash to the Philadelphia 76ers for Wilt Chamberlain. The Lakers now had a third superstar. And when they roared into the NBA Finals that season, some believed they were ready to turn the tables on the Celtics.

The series went to a dramatic Game 7. The Celtics took a 17-point lead early in the fourth quarter. Chamberlain hurt his knee a few minutes later and left the game. The Lakers appeared doomed.

Instead, they battled back. Chamberlain told coach Butch Van Breda Kolff he was ready to return to the game. But the coach, who often argued with Chamberlain, refused to put him back on the court. He told his future Hall of Fame center that the team was doing fine without him.

As Chamberlain sat angrily on the bench, the Lakers pulled

Most Valuable in Defeat

Lakers Hall of Fame guard Jerry West was mad and disgusted after being named the 1969 NBA Finals MVP. That is because his team lost the series to Boston. Through 2010–11, West remained the only player on a losing team to win NBA Finals MVP. He earned it after recording 42 points, 13 rebounds, and 12 assists in the Game 7 defeat.

to within two points. But the Celtics held on to beat the Lakers 108–106.

Despite winning the 1972 title over the New York Knicks, the pain of consistently losing to the Celtics would linger for another decade. It would take Kareem Abdul-Jabbar and a man called Magic to finally end the curse of the Celtics.

Lakers star Wilt Chamberlain prepares to shoot during a 1973 game.

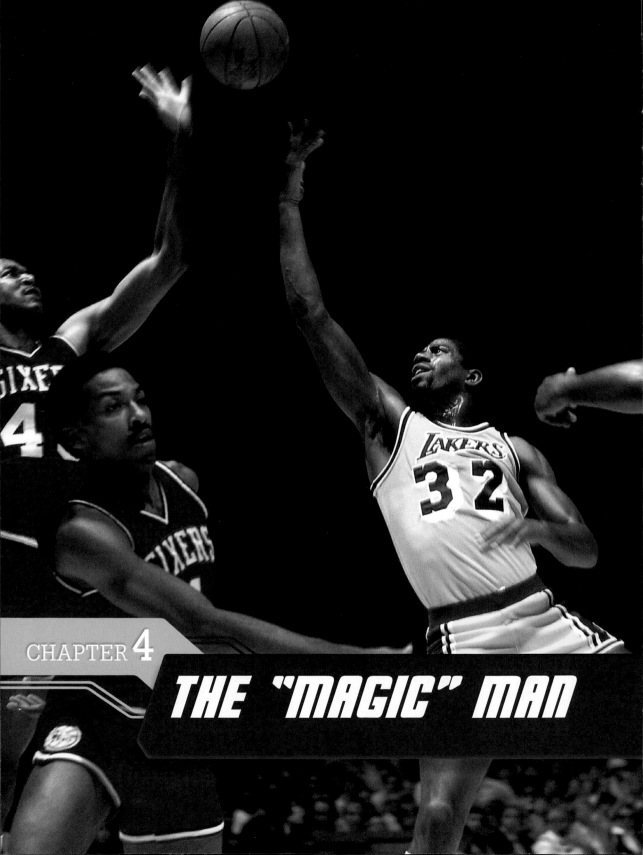

CHAPTER 4

THE "MAGIC" MAN

T he 1974–75 season featured an unusual ending for the Lakers. The end of the season was when they usually began preparing for the playoffs. But for the first time since the 1957–58 season, they were not in the postseason.

Wilt Chamberlain and Jerry West had retired. The only remaining star from the previously dominant Los Angeles team was Gail Goodrich. The Lakers were desperate to regain their place as championship contenders.

To do that, the Lakers wanted Kareem Abdul-Jabbar of the Milwaukee Bucks. The center was demanding a trade. He wanted to play in New York or Los Angeles, so it was a perfect fit. On June 16, 1975, the Lakers traded four players for Abdul-Jabbar.

Going to Milwaukee were promising center Elmore Smith, guard Brian Winters,

Magic Johnson (32) of the Los Angeles Lakers drives to the basket against the Philadelphia 76ers during an NBA game in 1981 in Los Angeles.

Individually, Abdul-Jabbar led the league in rebounding and blocked shots. He placed second in scoring. And he was named the NBA MVP. But as a team, the Lakers finished with just a 40–42 record. They again missed the playoffs.

West took over as coach during the offseason to try to turn around the team. Under his guidance, the Lakers responded in 1976–77 by recording a league-best 53–29 record. But the team still lost in the second round of the playoffs. They were eliminated quickly from the postseason the next two seasons, as well.

Goodrich left for the New Orleans Jazz as a free agent in 1978. The move would actually help the Lakers. New Orleans gave Los Angeles three college draft picks in return for signing Goodrich. And when the Jazz finished the 1978–79

and forwards Junior Bridge-man and Dave Meyers. The trade made the Bucks title con-tenders for years to come. They rose from last place in the Mid-west Division in 1975 to first in 1976.

The Lakers, on the other hand, did not experience such a quick turnaround. The addition of Abdul-Jabbar did not trans-form them into champions.

Lakers center Kareem Abdul-Jabbar, *left*, and Portland Trail Blazers center Bill Walton, *right*, battle for position during a playoff game in 1977.

season with the worst record in the NBA, it meant the Lakers would have the first choice in the 1979 NBA Draft.

The Lakers quickly chose a 6-foot-9 point guard out of Michigan State named Earvin Johnson. Basketball fans were amazed by his dribbling and passing skills. Those skills helped him earn his nickname— "Magic." The Lakers were once again about to become a dynasty.

Johnson and Abdul-Jabbar formed one of the best duos in

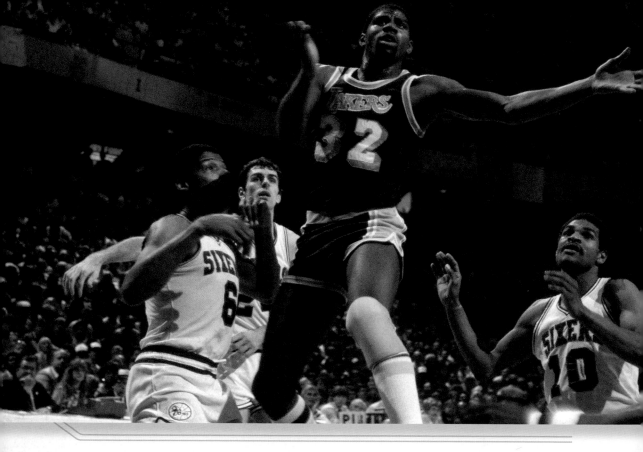

Lakers guard Earvin "Magic" Johnson (32) passes the ball against Philadelphia 76ers players during an NBA Finals game in 1980.

the league. But the Lakers were more than a two-man team. They also featured talented players such as high-scoring forward Jamaal Wilkes, defensive stalwart Michael Cooper, and steady guard Norm Nixon.

Johnson had an amazing rookie season. He led the Lakers into the 1980 NBA Finals, where they faced Julius Erving and the Philadelphia 76ers. Abdul-Jabbar scored 40 points in Game 5 to give the Lakers a 3–2 series lead. But he also sprained his ankle and could not play in Game 6.

The basketball world was shocked when Johnson stepped up and started at center instead of starting at point guard. But in an amazing NBA Finals performance, he posted 42 points, 15 rebounds, and seven assists in a 123–107 Lakers victory that clinched the title.

"It was amazing, just amazing," said Erving. "We went over everything they do when Kareem's not there, and we still couldn't do anything about it. . . . Magic was outstanding. Unreal."

The Lakers could not repeat as champions the next season. They lost in the first round of the 1981 playoffs. And when they started poorly the next year, owner Jerry Buss fired head coach Paul Westhead and promoted assistant Pat Riley. It proved to be the right move.

The Lakers were one of the best teams in the NBA over the next eight years with Riley as coach. In 1982, they lost

THE LIFE OF RILEY

The Lakers have produced some of the finest coaches in NBA history. Among them was Pat Riley. He began his career as a solid guard and forward for the San Diego Rockets in the late 1960s. He then played for the Lakers in the 1970s.

Named coach of the Lakers in 1981, he guided the team to championships in 1982, 1985, 1987, and 1988. He coached the New York Knicks for four seasons, leading them into the NBA Finals in 1994. He then became coach of the Miami Heat in 1995 and won the title in 2006. He was named NBA Coach of the Year in 1990, 1993, and 1997.

"He understands everybody," former Lakers point guard Earvin "Magic" Johnson said in 1987. "He understands you and knows how you are and treats a guy like he is. That's what he does best—he gets the most out of a guy because he understands him."

often one of the highest scoring in the NBA, and the most exciting to watch.

But the Lakers still had unfinished business. They had yet to forget all of those losses in the Finals to the Celtics in the 1950s and 1960s. The 1984 NBA Finals series was the first to feature the matchup between the Lakers' Johnson and the Celtics' superstar Larry Bird. The Celtics defeated the Lakers once again, this time in seven games.

The two teams faced each other again in the Finals the following season. Now 38 years old, Abdul-Jabbar still played like he was 28. He averaged more than 30 points and 11 rebounds per game in the series to carry Los Angeles to the title in six games. Abdul-Jabbar was named NBA Finals MVP. And the Lakers had finally beaten the Celtics for the title.

only two playoff games to roll to the championship over the 76ers. And thanks to an earlier trade with the Cleveland Cavaliers, Los Angeles had the first pick in the college draft that summer. They selected forward James Worthy, who would eventually be elected into the Hall of Fame.

Johnson's dazzling passes and Worthy's high-flying dunks helped start the "Showtime" era for the Lakers. They ran a fast-break offense that was

James Worthy of the Lakers grabs a rebound against the Detroit Pistons during a 1988 NBA Finals game at the Forum.

Los Angeles again beat the Celtics in the Finals two years later in 1987. And the Lakers then won a second straight championship by defeating the Detroit Pistons in the 1988 Finals. Worthy was the hero in that series. He had 36 points, 16 rebounds, and 10 assists in Game 7 to clinch the title.

But the Lakers' championship run would come to an end after that year. Abdul-Jabbar retired following the 1988–89 season. Two years later, Johnson made an announcement that would shock not only the basketball world, but the entire nation. And it would take years for the Lakers to recover.

CHAPTER 5

KOBE AND A NEW DYNASTY

Kareem Abdul-Jabbar had dominated NBA opponents for 19 years. His sky-hook, which many consider one of the toughest shots to defend in NBA history, had become legendary. It was nearly impossible to block.

But Abdul-Jabbar was 41 years old at the start of the 1988–89 season. He knew he had played long enough. So the center announced he would retire at the end of the season. He tried to leave the game by winning one more NBA title. But his Lakers were swept in the Finals by the Detroit Pistons.

The next year, the Lakers were upset in the second round of the playoffs. Pat Riley quit as coach after that season and was replaced by Mike Dunleavy. Dunleavy guided Los Angeles to the 1991 NBA Finals. The Lakers won Game 1, but then lost four straight games as the Chicago Bulls won the title. Then came news at the start of

Lakers guard Kobe Bryant dunks during a game against the Minnesota Timberwolves in 2011.

Lakers center Shaquille O'Neal, *left*, drives on Boston Celtics forward Frank Brickowski during a game in Boston in 1996.

the following season that surprised everyone.

Only three games into the 1991–92 season, Magic Johnson announced his retirement. He told a national television audience that he was sick. He had been diagnosed with human immunodeficiency virus (HIV), which can be deadly.

Despite the loss of Johnson, the Lakers squeaked into the playoffs. They were eliminated in the first round by the Portland Trail Blazers. In 1992–93, Los Angeles finished with a losing record and again lost in the first round of the playoffs. The Lakers then struggled to a 33–49 record in 1993–94 and missed the playoffs completely.

The team had no superstar. So, in 1996, Los Angeles spent millions of dollars to get one.

The Lakers understood they had enjoyed their greatest success when they had great centers. Wilt Chamberlain and Abdul-Jabbar had led them to titles. So they signed free agent Shaquille O'Neal. The dominant center was 7 feet 1 inch and weighed 350 pounds. But he was quick for his size.

O'Neal missed 31 games in his first year with the Lakers due to a knee injury. When healthy, he averaged 26.2 points and 12.5 rebounds per game. O'Neal was the superstar Los Angeles wanted. But the Lakers had another player on the team who would also become a superstar.

Days before signing O'Neal, the Lakers traded center Vlade Divac to the Charlotte Hornets. In return, they got an 18-year-old high-school player that Charlotte had drafted with the 13th pick

THE SHAQ-KOBE FEUD

Those who watched Kobe Bryant and Shaquille O'Neal play together could not imagine a problem developing between the two. But the relationship came apart before the 2003–04 season. O'Neal told the media that Bryant needed to pass the ball more. Bryant replied that O'Neal should only worry about himself.

Their disagreement became worse as the season progressed. O'Neal decided to leave Los Angeles, and he was traded to the Miami Heat for the 2004–05 season. He went on to win a title with the Heat in 2005–06. Bryant spent the next several years trying to prove he could do the same without O'Neal. He admitted after winning a title in 2009 that the task had been tough.

He said. "I was just like, it's a challenge I'm just going to have to accept, because there's no way to argue it. . . . It's not going anywhere until you do something about it."

in the 1996 NBA draft. That player was guard Kobe Bryant. The pairing of O'Neal and Bryant turned the Lakers into instant winners. Bryant turned 21 during the 1999–2000 season and was already one of the league's top players.

That same year, Los Angeles hired Phil Jackson, who had guided the legendary Michael Jordan and the Chicago Bulls to six titles in the 1990s. The Lakers finished the season 67–15, which was their best record in 28 years. But they received a scare from Portland in the Western Conference finals. Los Angeles trailed by 13 points in the deciding Game 7 before staging an incredible comeback to win. The Lakers then dominated the Indiana Pacers in the Finals to claim their first NBA championship since 1988.

The Lakers were once again the best team in the league.

The Greatest Coach Ever?

Phil Jackson has been fortunate to have coached three superstars: Michael Jordan in Chicago and Kobe Bryant and Shaquille O'Neal in Los Angeles. But he still had to mold all of that talent in order to win titles. That is why some believe he is the finest NBA coach ever. Jackson owns the league record for most championships with 11. He won six with the Bulls and five more with the Lakers.

During the next two years, they cruised to NBA Finals victories over the Philadelphia 76ers and the New Jersey Nets. That gave the team three consecutive titles for the first time in franchise history.

The Lakers' championship streak ended the following year with a loss to the Detroit Pistons in the 2004 Finals. O'Neal was traded to the Miami Heat during the offseason. It took several years for Los Angeles to recover. In early 2008, however, they traded for 7-foot

The Lakers' Kobe Bryant, *left*, and Shaquille O'Neal led their team to a Game 5 victory in the 2002 Western Conference semifinals.

forward-center Pau Gasol. That began their resurgence.

With Bryant and Gasol leading the way, the Lakers advanced to the 2009 NBA Finals. But it was not one of the team's stars who made the big shots to bring the championship back to Los Angeles. It was a guard named Derek Fisher.

The Lakers built a 2–1 series lead against the Orlando Magic in the Finals. The Magic were poised to tie the series. They held a five-point lead in the final minute of Game 4. But Fisher sank two clutch three-pointers for Los Angeles. The first sent the game into overtime. The second gave his Lakers the victory. They clinched the title in Game 5 three days later with a 99–86 win. Bryant was named the

Finals MVP for averaging 32.4 points and 7.4 assists per game for the series. But Fisher was the real hero.

The Lakers and their fans were proud of the four titles they had won since 2000. But none of those titles had come against the Boston Celtics, their heated rivals. In fact, Los Angeles lost to Boston again in the 2008 NBA Finals.

The Lakers got another chance in 2010. The Finals series came down to a dramatic Game 7 in Los Angeles for the championship. The Lakers fell behind by 13 points in the third quarter. But they stormed back. When forward Ron Artest hit a three-pointer with one minute remaining, the Lakers held a 79–73 lead. They hung on to clinch an 83–79 victory and the NBA title.

"This one's by far the sweetest," Bryant said. The Lakers

now owned back-to-back titles. And the team was determined to win a third straight championship in 2011. Los Angeles finished the season 57–25 to enter the playoffs as the second seed in the Western Conference.

The Lakers faced the New Orleans Hornets in the first round. The Hornets surprised the Lakers by winning Game 1 in Los Angeles. But the Lakers regrouped to win four of the next five games and take the series.

Los Angeles faced the Dallas Mavericks in the second round. Like New Orleans, the

The Lakers' Derek Fisher (2) drives on Boston Celtics players Kevin Garnett (5) and Ray Allen (20) during Game 5 of the 2010 NBA Finals.

Mavericks beat the Lakers in Game 1, 96–94 in Los Angeles. But the Lakers were not able to regroup as they had against the Hornets. Dallas won Game 2 93–81, and then won Game 3 98–92 in Dallas. The Lakers quest for a third straight title was on the line in Game 4.

The game was close at the end of the first quarter. But Dallas outscored the Lakers by 20 points in the second quarter to take control of the game. The Lakers lost 122–86. It was a tough way to end the season. But with players such as Bryant and Gasol leading the way, fans hope the Lakers can regroup to win a 16th NBA championship.

TIMELINE

1947 The Detroit Gems move to Minneapolis and become the Lakers. The end of the PBLA results in the Lakers signing future Hall of Fame center George Mikan.

1948 The Lakers defeat the Rochester Royals to win the NBL title in their first year in the league.

1950 The Lakers clinch their first NBA championship on April 23 with a 110–95 victory over the Syracuse Nationals in Game 6 of the Finals.

1954 The Lakers secure their fourth title in five years on April 12 with an 87–80 defeat of Syracuse in Game 7 of the Finals.

1958 Hall of Fame forward Elgin Baylor is drafted by the Lakers on April 22.

1960 Guard Jerry West is selected by the Lakers with the second overall pick in the NBA Draft on April 11. Owner Bob Short announces on April 28 he is moving the franchise from Minneapolis to Los Angeles.

1962 On April 18, the Lakers lose Game 7 of the NBA Finals to Boston in overtime 110–107. A Frank Selvy shot that could have won the game hits off the rim.

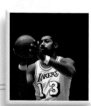

1968 Hall of Fame center Wilt Chamberlain is traded from the Philadelphia 76ers to the Lakers on July 9.

1972 The Lakers' league-record 33-game winning streak is halted on January 9 by the Milwaukee Bucks on national TV. The Lakers clinch their first NBA title since moving to Los Angeles with a 114–100 win over New York on May 7.

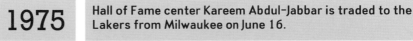

1975	Hall of Fame center Kareem Abdul-Jabbar is traded to the Lakers from Milwaukee on June 16.
1979	The Lakers choose Hall of Fame guard Earvin "Magic" Johnson with the first overall pick of the NBA Draft on June 25.
1985	Avenging eight Finals losses to Boston since 1959, the Lakers beat the Celtics for the title. The championship is clinched with a 111–100 victory on June 9.

1988	The Lakers secure their third NBA title in four years on June 21 with a 108-105 defeat of the Detroit Pistons in Game 7 of the Finals.
1996	Superstar Kobe Bryant is acquired by the Lakers on July 11 from the Charlotte Hornets. On July 18, the Lakers sign free agent center Shaquille O'Neal.
1999	Phil Jackson becomes the new Lakers coach on July 16.

2002	The Lakers clinch a third straight title for the first time in franchise history. They complete an NBA Finals sweep of the New Jersey Nets with a 113–107 win on June 12.
2004	A feud between Kobe Bryant and Shaquille O'Neal forces the Lakers to trade O'Neal to the Miami Heat on July 14.
2010	The Lakers clinch their second straight NBA title on June 17 with an 83–79 win over Boston in Game 7 of the Finals.

QUICK STATS

FRANCHISE HISTORY

Minneapolis Lakers (1947–60)
Los Angeles Lakers (1960–)

NBA FINALS
(wins in bold)

1950, **1952**, **1953**, **1954**, 1959, 1962,
1963, 1965, 1966, 1968, 1969, 1970,
1972, 1973, **1980**, **1982**, 1983, 1984,
1985, **1987**, **1988**, 1989, 1991, **2000**,
2001, **2002**, 2004, 2008, **2009**, **2010**

KEY PLAYERS
(position[s]; years with the team)

Kareem Abdul-Jabbar (C; 1975–89)
Elgin Baylor (F; 1958–71)
Kobe Bryant (G; 1996–)
Wilt Chamberlain (C; 1968–73)

Pau Gasol (F; 2008–)
Gail Goodrich (G; 1965–68, 1970–76)
Earvin "Magic" Johnson (G; 1979–91,
    1995–96)
Clyde Lovellette (F/C; 1953–57)
Slater Martin (G; 1949–56)
George Mikan (C; 1948–54, 1955–56)
Vern Mikkelsen (F; 1949–59)
Lamar Odom (F; 2004–)
Shaquille O'Neal (C; 1996–2004)
Jim Pollard (F; 1948–55)
Jerry West (G; 1960–74)
James Worthy (F; 1982–94)

KEY COACHES

Phil Jackson (1999–2004, 2005–11):
    610–292; 118–63 (postseason)
John Kundla (1948–59):
    423–302; 60–35 (postseason)
Pat Riley (1981–90):
    533–194; 102–47 (postseason)

HOME ARENAS

Minneapolis Auditorium (1947–60)
Los Angeles Memorial Sports Arena
    (1960–67)
The Forum (1967–99)
Staples Center (1999–)

* All statistics through 2010–11 season

QUOTES AND ANECDOTES

Since the Lakers play so close to Hollywood, there has been a close connection between the franchise and the entertainment world. Not only do many celebrities regularly attend home games, but they have also developed relationships with players. One example involves Khloe Kardashian. The reality TV star married Lakers forward Lamar Odom in the fall of 2009.

The Lakers had just compiled a disturbing 33–49 record in 1994. It was their worst season in 18 years. They were so desperate that they fired coach Randy Pfund and replaced him with Magic Johnson. But the Lakers lacked talent and a 10-game losing streak followed. Johnson announced after the season that he would not return as coach. There was no magic—or "Magic"—left in Los Angeles.

Lakers players have come and gone, but announcer Chick Hearn was a mainstay with the organization for more than 40 years. Hearn began broadcasting Lakers games when they moved to Los Angeles from Minneapolis in 1960. He broadcast an incredible 3,338 consecutive Lakers games from 1965 to 2001. Hearn died at age 85 in 2002.

"He was making the kind of moves I'd never seen from a player his size. He was dribbling the length of the floor, looking one way and passing another. He was hitting every open man, making all the right decisions. Basically, he was controlling the entire game. He was their unmistakable leader. I was astounded." —Lakers general manager Jerry West after watching Michigan State freshman Magic Johnson perform

GLOSSARY

assist

A pass that leads directly to a made basket.

draft

A system used by professional sports leagues to select new players in order to spread incoming talent among all teams. The NBA Draft is held each June.

dynasty

A team that dominates a particular league or sport for a period of time.

fast break

A style of basketball in which a team runs down the court and tries to score before the opponent's defense is set.

franchise

An entire sports organization, including the players, coaches, and staff.

free agent

A player whose contract has expired and who is able to sign with a team of his choice.

general manager

The executive who is in charge of the team's overall operation. He or she hires and fires coaches, drafts players, and signs free agents.

postseason

The games in which the best teams play after the regular-season schedule has been completed.

rebound

To secure the basketball after a missed shot.

rookie

An athlete playing in his first year in a professional league.

trade

A move in which a player or players are sent from one team to another.

upset

A victory by a team that is not expected to win over a superior opponent.

FOR MORE INFORMATION

Further Reading

Ballard, Chris. *The Art of a Beautiful Game: The Thinking Fan's Tour of the NBA*. New York, NY: Simon & Schuster, 2009.

Doeden, Matt. *Wilt Chamberlain (Sports Heroes and Legends)*. Breckenridge, CO: Twenty-First Century Books, 2010.

Simmons, Bill. *The Book of Basketball: The NBA According to the Sports Guy*. New York, NY: Random House, 2009.

Web Links

To learn more about the Los Angeles Lakers, visit ABDO Publishing Company online at **www.abdopublishing.com**. Web sites about the Lakers are featured on our Book Links page. These links are routinely monitored and updated to provide the most current information available.

Places To Visit

Naismith Memorial Basketball Hall of Fame
1000 West Columbus Avenue
Springfield, MA 01105
413-781-6500
www.hoophall.com
This hall of fame and museum highlights the greatest players and moments in the history of basketball. Wilt Chamberlain, Jerry West, Kareem Abdul-Jabbar, and Magic Johnson are among the former Lakers enshrined here.

Sports Museum of Los Angeles
1111 South Figueroa Street
Los Angeles, CA 90015
213-742-7326
www.staplescenter.com
The Sports Museum of Los Angeles is located inside of Staples Center. Fans can visit before and during all Lakers games. The museum is located on the main concourse.

Staples Center
1111 South Figueroa Street
Los Angeles, CA 90015
213-742-7326
www.staplescenter.com
This has been the Lakers' home arena since 1999. The team plays 41 regular season games here each year.

INDEX

About the Author

Marty Gitlin is a freelance writer based in Cleveland, Ohio. He has written more than 35 educational books. He has also won more than 45 awards during his 25 years as a writer, including first place for general excellence from the *Associated Press*. Gitlin lives with his wife and three children.